Portage Public Library

DISCARDED

Stickleback Fish

First Steck-Vaughn Edition 1992

This book has been reviewed
for accuracy by
David Skryja
Associate Professor of Biology
University of Wisconsin Center—Waukesha.

Library of Congress Cataloging in Publication Data

Pohl, Kathleen.
　　Stickleback fish.

　　(Nature close-ups)
　　Adaptation of: Togeuo / Hidetomo Oda and Atsushi Sakurai.
　　Summary: Describes in text and photographs the life cycle and behavior patterns of the stickleback fish.
　　1. Sticklebacks—juvenile literature.　[1. Sticklebacks.
2. Fishes]　I. Oda, Hidetomo. Togeuo.　II. Title.
III. Series.
QL638.G27P65　　1986　　　597′.53　　86-26314

ISBN 0-8172-2722-9 (lib. bdg.)
ISBN 0-8172-2740-7 (softcover)

This edition first published in 1987 by Raintree Publishers Inc., a Division of Steck-Vaughn Company.

Text copyright © 1987 by Raintree Publishers Inc., translated by Jun Amano from *The Stickle Back* copyright © 1984 by Hidetomo Oda and Atsushi Sakurai.

Photographs copyright © 1984 by Atsushi Sakurai.

World English translation rights for *Color Photo Books on Nature* arranged with Kaisei-Sha through Japan Foreign-Rights Center.

All rights reserved. No part of the material protected by this copyright may be reproduced or utilized in any form by any means, electronic or mechanical, including photocopying, recording, or by any information storage and retrieval system, without permission in writing from Steck-Vaughn Company, P.O. Box 26015, Austin, TX 78755. Printed in the United States of America.

2 3 4 5 6 7 8 9 0　　　95 94 93 92

Stickleback Fish
Adapted by
Kathleen Pohl

RAINTREE
STECK-VAUGHN
PUBLISHERS
The Steck-Vaughn Company

Austin, Texas

◀ **A stream in spring.**

Some sticklebacks live in rivers and streams like this one. Others live in the ocean but swim to fresh water to lay their eggs.

▶ **A school of stickleback fish.**

Most sticklebacks are only a few inches long. The males and females of the same species look a lot alike, except during the mating season. This species is greenish black with silvery sides.

Thousands of different kinds of fish live in the oceans and in freshwater lakes and streams throughout the world. Among them are stickleback fish. It is easy to tell sticklebacks from other fish because they have sharp spines on their back. These spines help to protect the stickleback from enemies. Sticklebacks may have three or four spines, or as many as twelve. The number varies, depending on the kind, or species, of stickleback.

During much of the year, male and female sticklebacks swim together in groups, called schools. But in spring, as the water begins to warm up, the male stickleback leaves the school. The mating season is nearing, and he must prepare to become a father. For as you will see, the male stickleback is one of the best of all fathers in the fish world.

● **Varieties of sticklebacks.**

The species of stickleback on the left averages seven to twelve small spines. Each of the two sticklebacks at the right has three large spines.

▲ A female (top) and male three-spined stickleback during the mating season.

▲ A male (top) and female ten-spined stickleback during the mating season.

At most times of the year, male sticklebacks are the same color as females. But during the mating season, the male turns a different color to attract females of his species. The mating colors of the male vary from species to species. The three-spined stickleback turns bright red along his throat and belly, and his eyes become a brilliant blue. The ten-spined stickleback, also shown in these photos, turns a deep black, especially on his underside.

Once the male stickleback has left his school, he searches for a suitable place to build a nest. Three-spined sticklebacks choose a shallow pool of water or a stream with a sandy bottom. The ten-spined stickleback chooses a place where water plants thrive. Once the stickleback has found a place to nest, he chases off other males that swim near. In this way, the male stickleback defends his territory.

◀ A fight over territory.

Once a male stickleback has found a suitable nest site, he will fight to defend it if another male stickleback comes near.

▼ **A male stickleback driving another male away from his territory.**

A male stickleback becomes very defensive if another male swims into his territory. This stickleback has raised his spines to frighten off another male.

◀ **A stickleback carrying a piece of water plant to the nest site.**

When the tiny nest is finished, it will look something like a bird's nest. It will measure an inch and a half to two inches in diameter.

▶ **A stickleback binding his nest together.**

After the stickleback has formed his nest, he swims around it, secreting a sticky mucus. The mucus binds the plant pieces together, so that the nest will not break apart.

The male ten-spined stickleback makes his nest at the roots of water plants. He bites off tiny pieces of plant roots and stems and carries them to the nest site. He binds the pieces together with a sticky fluid, mucus, which he secretes from his kidneys. Then he gathers sand from the bottom of the pond or lake and uses it to make the nest stronger. Finally, the male stickleback lines the inside of the nest with soft moss or algae. When the tiny nest is completed, it has a tunnel-like opening with an entrance at either end. It takes about a day for this species of stickleback to complete a nest.

◀ **A stickleback adding mucus to his nest (left) and checking it over (right).**

The male stickleback checks his nest many times before it is completed. When he is all finished building it, he swims through it to check it one final time.

▲ **A stickleback digging a hole.**

The male sucks up sand with his mouth and spits it out nearby. When the hole is deep enough, he begins to anchor plant pieces there.

▲ **A stickleback spitting out sand.**

The male sucks up sand and spits it out over and over again. This species makes holes about an inch deep and four inches across.

The male three-spined stickleback builds his nest in a somewhat different way. He begins by making a hole in the sandy bottom of a lake or pond. He does this by sucking up mouthfuls of sand and spitting it out. The male does this many times until he has dug a hole large enough to anchor the nest. If another stickleback comes near during this time, the one building the nest will stand on his head, suck up sand and blow it out in clouds to scare off the visitor.

When the hole is deep enough, the stickleback begins to collect sticks and roots and bits of water plants. He carries them to the hole and arranges them there. Then he swims around the nest materials, secreting mucus which binds them together. When he is all done, the male stickleback swims through the tunnel-like nest to look it over.

◀ **A three-spined stickleback checking his nest.**

When the nest is completed, the male swims through it to check it.

▼ **A three-spined stickleback carrying plant roots to his nest site.**

After he has dug his hole, the male stickleback collects pieces of water plants and brings them to the nest site.

▲ **A male stickleback (bottom) zigzagging around a female.**
The male darts in and out as he swims near the female during his courtship dance.

▲ **A male stickleback (bottom) leading a female to his nest.**
The female responds to the male's dance by showing him her abdomen. Then he leads her to the nest.

Once the male stickleback has completed his nest, he is ready to mate. Females of his species are attracted to him because of his bright mating colors. If a thin female swims near, the male will ignore her. He knows that a thin female cannot be carrying eggs. But when he sees a female with a fat abdomen bulging with eggs, he will be attracted to her. Then he begins a courtship dance.

He zigzags around her and tries to lead her to his nest. At first, she might not seem interested. He may have to repeat the zigzag dance several times. Eventually, she will swim with him to the nest. He shows her the entrance by poking his snout into it.

◀ **A male stickleback attacking a female.**
If a female swims into a male's territory before he has completed his nest, he will drive her away.

▼ **A male stickleback showing a female the entrance to his nest.**

If a female is not ready to mate, she will swim away from the male. But if she is ready, she follows him to the nest site and he shows her the entrance. He may prod her with his spines if she is too slow.

◀ **A female stickleback laying her eggs.**

Because the female's abdomen is so swollen with eggs, it is hard for her to work her way into the nest. But once she is inside, it takes less than a minute for her to spawn.

▶ **A male stickleback nudging a female.**

The female's tail sticks out of the nest just far enough so that the male can nudge her. Soon she begins to lay her eggs.

When the female stickleback enters the nest, her body is sheltered except for her head and tail, which stick out at either end of the tunnel. The male nudges her tail with his snout, moving it back and forth rapidly. She responds to this movement by laying a mass of jellylike eggs in the nest. This is called spawning. She may lay as many as 100 eggs in less than a minute. Then she leaves the nest, and the male enters. He swims through the tunnel, spraying the eggs with his sperm. This fertilizes the eggs, and baby sticklebacks begin to grow inside.

▼ **A male fertilizing the eggs.**

As soon as the female stickleback leaves the nest, the male swims through it, fertilizing the eggs with his sperm.

◀ **A male ten-spined stickleback leading a female to his nest.**

This male does a zigzag dance to lead the female to his nest at the base of water plants.

▶ **Close-up of a stickleback's eggs inside a nest.**

The eggs stick together in a jelly-like mass inside the nest.

Once the female stickleback has laid her eggs, she is very thin. The male is no longer attracted to her. She swims away from the nest, or he may chase her off.

The male may invite other females to his nest to lay their eggs. This ten-spined stickleback makes a nest large enough to hold a thousand eggs at one time. As the eggs develop, tiny fish embryos form inside the egg cases. The embryos develop at slightly different rates because the eggs were laid at different times by the female sticklebacks.

◀ **A male stickleback encouraging a female to lay her eggs.**

When the nest becomes full of eggs, this male stickleback will narrow the entrance to the nest to protect the eggs.

◀ **Embryos beginning to develop inside the eggs.**

If more than one female lays her eggs in the nest, the embryos will mature at slightly different times.

▶ **A stickleback sending fresh water to the eggs.**

This male uses his pectoral fins to send fresh water into the nest. Oxygen is absorbed by the embryos through the egg cases.

The male stickleback stands guard over the nest until the eggs hatch. If fish or other animals come near, the stickleback may suck up a mouthful of sand and spit it out at them to scare them away. Or he may raise his spines to frighten an enemy that threatens his eggs.

The male stickleback also takes care of the eggs. He uses his front fins, his pectoral fins, to fan water into the tunnel of the nest, sending fresh oxygen to the eggs. This constant supply of water also keeps the eggs fresh and clean.

And from time to time, the male will bring mouthfuls of sand to the nest to strengthen it while the tiny fish embryos are growing inside.

▲ **A three-spined stickleback (left) and a ten-spined stickleback (right) fanning fresh water to their eggs.**

▲ **Eggs in which embryos are forming.**
By the fifth day, the black eyes of the embryos can be seen through the egg cases.

▲ **A newly hatched stickleback.**
The baby stickleback has a yolk sac attached to its stomach. It does not look at all like an adult stickleback.

Within five days, the embryo's black eyes become visible through the egg case. Its tiny heart and long tail have formed. Ten or twelve days after the eggs are laid, they are ready to hatch. The embryos break through the egg cases. The tiny, newborn fish are called fry. At first, their fins and mouths are not fully developed. The fry cannot swim well. Large yolk sacs remain attached to their stomachs. These provide nutrition for the fry for several more days. During this time, the fry remain close to the nest or hidden among water plants.

◀ **A baby stickleback feeding on the egg yolk.**
For several days, the young stickleback feeds on the egg yolk. Then it begins to search for food on its own.

▼ **Stickleback fry hanging from their nest.** The newly hatched fry cannot swim at first. They move jerkily through the water. These fry are hanging from the sticks and leaves of their nest.

◄ **A baby stickleback looking for food.**

Once its yolk sac is used up, the young stickleback begins to search for food on its own. Its huge eyes help it to spot tiny animal prey.

► **A young stickleback swimming.**

At this stage of growth, the young stickleback's head looks too large for its body. But it already has fins and spines and resembles an adult.

The male stickleback guards the nest and watches over the stickleback fry until they are about two weeks old. During this time, if a baby stickleback tries to leave the nest, the father will swim after it, suck it into his mouth, and spit it out again in the nest. If an animal threatens the fry, the male will attack it. Hungry fish and birds like to hunt, or prey upon, young sticklebacks.

Soon the young fry become better swimmers. They begin to leave the nest in groups and are able to survive on their own. They swim around, searching for mosquito larvae, water fleas, and tiny worms to eat.

With his job done, the male stickleback gradually loses his nesting and fathering instincts—until the next mating season.

◄ **A male (left) and female stickleback (right) searching for food.**

Sticklebacks prefer animal protein, rather than plants. When they are very young, they eat plankton, tiny bits of animal matter that float in the water. As they grow older, they eat worms and mosquito larvae.

◀ **A group of sticklebacks among water plants.**

Sticklebacks swim by themselves when they are searching for food. But when they sense danger, they gather in schools.

▶ **A spring-fed pond (above) and sticklebacks swimming in a school (below).**

The temperature remains fairly constant in spring-fed ponds. Even in winter, they do not freeze over. Some species of sticklebacks spend the winter in such ponds.

Gradually, the male stickleback loses his brilliant mating colors. By winter, he has returned to his original color and again looks like the females of his species. He again joins a school of sticklebacks and they swim together for safety.

The young sticklebacks that have survived the dangerous early stages of their lives now also swim together in schools. Some species of sticklebacks mature in about a year's time. It takes other species two or three years before the males are ready to begin their role as fathers in the fish world.

◀ **A male stickleback that has lost his mating colors.**

Except during the mating season, it is not easy to tell male and female sticklebacks apart.

▶ **A male goby protecting eggs hanging from a rock.**

These tiny embryos are nearly two weeks old. They are just about ready to hatch. Notice their huge black eyes and long tails.

◀ **Newly hatched goby fry.**

The male goby licks the egg cases just as the fry are ready to hatch. The tiny fry break through the egg cases and swim out into the water.

Like the sticklebacks, some male goby fish play a role in hatching the eggs. The male of this species stakes out his territory in shallow waters. He chooses a nest site beneath a stone or rock and makes a hole. The female goby lays her eggs there, attaching them to the rock with a sticky substance. This helps to keep the eggs from being washed away by the current.

The male goby keeps watch nearby to protect the eggs from enemies. He fans his pectoral fins to send fresh water over the developing embryos. When they are ready to hatch, the male goby of this species gently nibbles the egg cases. This helps the tiny fry to hatch from the eggs.

◀ **An adult goby on a river bottom.**

The goby's mottled colors blend in with the stones on this river bottom, helping to keep the fish hidden from enemies. Adult gobies of this species grow as long as five inches.

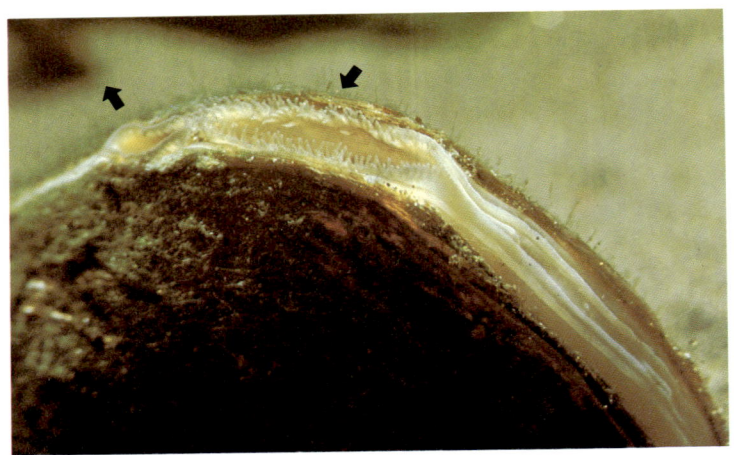

▶ **Bitterlings laying their eggs.**

The male bitterling picks a territory near mussels. Once a male finds a suitable mussel, the female pokes her long, curved ovipositor between the halves of the mussel shell and lays her eggs.

◀ **A mussel.**

The right arrow shows where the mussel takes in water; the left arrow shows where water is discharged from the mussel's shell.

But most male fish do not make such good fathers. So some fish depend on other animals to help protect their eggs.

Japanese and European bitterlings look for freshwater mussels in which to lay their eggs. The female bitterling has a long egg-laying tube, called an ovipositor, which she pokes between the two halves of the mussel's shell. She deposits her eggs in the gill chambers.

Then the male discharges his sperm into the water near the mussel. The water and the sperm are taken into the mussel's gills. The sperm joins with the eggs, fertilizing them. Water constantly washes over the gill chambers, bringing supplies of fresh oxygen to the eggs.

▼ **Eggs laid on the mussel's gills.**

The Japanese bitterling's eggs are whitish-yellow and long. They grow large enough to hatch in about four days.

▼ **Bitterling fry growing in the gills.**

The newly hatched fry are nourished by the yolk sac attached to their stomachs. In about three weeks, the fry are ready to leave the gills.

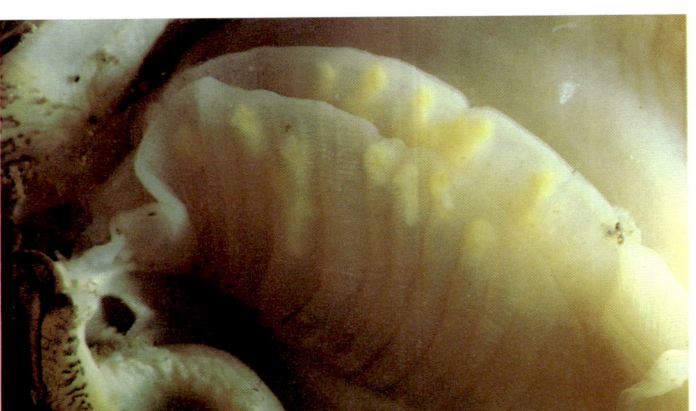

▼ A female bitterling laying her eggs.

▼ A male bitterling fertilizing the eggs.

Let's Find Out How to Raise Sticklebacks.

(**1**) A child catching sticklebacks in springtime. (**2**) A male stickleback with his mating colors. (**3**) A fat female stickleback carrying her eggs.

Look for sticklebacks in April and May, as the water begins to warm up in ponds and streams. Use a net to scoop up the fish. Put them in an aquarium. Add pond water. Be sure to keep the water temperature at 70 degrees Fahrenheit or less.

Add plants and sand to the aquarium. Feed your sticklebacks water worms and mosquito larvae. If you have caught both male and female sticklebacks, you will be able to watch the male build a nest and the female lay her eggs.

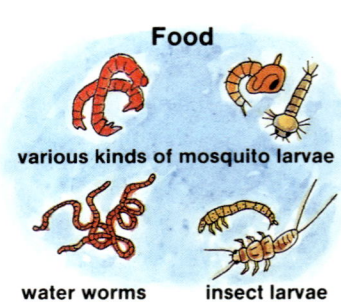

Watch the Male Fight.

When the male stickleback has chosen a nest site, place a mirror in your aquarium. He will see his own reflection and try to attack it, thinking it is an enemy.

A stickleback attacking his reflection in a mirror.

Watch How the Male Builds a Nest.

The male gathers plant roots and pond scum to build his nest. He binds the materials together with a sticky substance that he secretes from his kidneys.

A stickleback building his nest.

Watch How the Sticklebacks Court.

The male will do a zigzag dance around the female. She will lift her head and show her abdomen in response to the male's courtship dance.

A male showing a female the entrance to the nest.

Watch How the Male Cares for the Eggs.

After the eggs are laid, the male will care for them. He sends fresh water to the eggs so they can breathe. When the eggs hatch, the male also cares for the young fry for several days.

A male fanning fresh water to the eggs.

GLOSSARY

egg—a mature female germ cell. (pp. 15, 16, 18)

embryo—the early stages of development of a stickleback or other organism. (pp. 16, 18, 20)

fertilized—when a sperm and an egg unite, making it possible for a new organism to form. (p. 15)

fry—newly hatched fish. (pp. 20, 22)

instinct—behavior with which an animal is born, rather than behavior which is learned. (p. 22)

mating colors—the different colors that male sticklebacks take on during the mating season to attract females. (pp. 6, 24)

mucus—the sticky fluid which the male stickleback secretes from his kidneys to bind his nest together. (pp. 8, 10)

school—a large number of fish of one kind swimming together. (pp. 4, 6, 24)

spawning—releasing large numbers of eggs into the water at one time. Fish, frogs, and toads all spawn. (p. 15)

species—a group of animals which scientists have identified as having common traits. (pp. 4, 10)

territory—an area claimed by a male stickleback for nesting and mating purposes. (pp. 6, 7, 12)